THE SHINE POEMS

CALVIN FORBES

Louisiana State University Press *Baton Rouge*

2001

For BJ: the real poet in the family

Wheaton College, Norton, MA 02766

Copyright © 1979, 1980, 1981, 1992, 1994, 1995, 1996, 1997, 1998, 2001 by
    Calvin Forbes
All rights reserved
Manufactured in the United States of America

First printing
10 09 08 07 06 05 04 03 02 01
5 4 3 2 1

Designer: Amanda McDonald Scallan
Typeface: Sabon
Printer and binder: Thomson-Shore, Inc.

Library of Congress Cataloging-in-Publication Data:
Forbes, Calvin, 1945–
    The shine poems / Calvin Forbes.
        p. cm.
    ISBN 0-8071-2666-7 (alk. paper) —ISBN 0-8071-2667-5 (pbk. : alk. paper)
    I. Title.
    PS3556.O66 S55 2001
    811'.54—dc21

                                                                00-011231

Grateful acknowledgment is made to the editors of the following publications, in which
some of the poems herein first appeared: *Chicago Review:* "Two Children's Songs"; *Crab
Orchard Review:* "Church," "Funk Heart"; *Another Chicago Magazine:* "Two Moments";
New Virginia Review: "Blues"; *Jackleg:* "Two Songs"; *Planet: The Welsh Internationalist:*
"Kindness"; *Prairie Schooner:* "The Plea"; *The Southern Review:* "Namesake."
"Picture of a Man" was originally published in *In Search of Color Everywhere,* ed. E.
Ethelbert Miller (New York: Stewart, Tabori, and Chang, 1994).
The poems in part 4 were originally published as a chapbook, *From the Book of Shine*
(Providence, R.I.: Burning Deck Press, 1979; Wales, U.K.: Razorback Press, 1980).
The author would also like to acknowledge the assistance provided by a fellowship from
the Illinois Arts Council.

The paper in this book meets the guidelines for permanence and durability of the
Committee on Production Guidelines for Book Longevity of the Council on Library
Resources. ∞

CONTENTS

I

THE BIRTHDAY GIFT

you're not too old for a tree she said
smiling because it was obvious
I was far from a tree

we left the monkey out of the equation
through the window
sunlight like a beacon beckons

first there's the morning paper
apples biscuits green tea minor wonders
of civilization meanwhile

out there unlikely dissenters
whom we eavesdrop on
an uprising a riot of birds yakking

telegrams arrive like temptations
friends call to buoy the birthday boy
remember remember

you're the same age you'll be tomorrow
true 364 days out the year
as desirable as a yearly checkup

as for those trees you so admire
every time a big one falls please warn
the small and slow

THREE FOLK SONGS

1
my stonehenge a pile of rocks
primitive as a sandbox
the last primitive man
walking without a walkman

2
one death reminds me of another
this way I never forget
good poems are like some people
sometimes I can't remember their names
only how they made me feel

3
let's pray jesse helms
believes in hell
and that hell's paved
in porno zines

1967

some Angel's out of jail
so there's a party
for the Hell's Angels
at the Filmore

choppers line the curb
inside beer on the floor
blond hair in a fist
I keep my peace

a giant hash pipe floats by
its bowl round as a bear hug
Janis Joplin's on stage
Jefferson Airplane's in the wings

a lone dancer smiles to herself
I pretend to be speechless
years later words still fail me
yet it's true I was there

Self Portrait at Forty-Something

ears that stick out like Dr. Spock's
used to be embarrassing
a flat nose a cauliflower nose

not from punches
if anything from too much sneezing
black bearded short haired

only one other area processes
more significant hair
and he has not seen his chin in years

nor his cheeks undoubtedly
more rounded: the eyes
still that starved look about them

brown as his people's
are wont to be
muddy rivers beneath the cliff

of his brow which is gutted
erosion perhaps
with eyebrows raised like scars

no like squirrels really who scatter
into the waiting trees
he is left guessing as we are

NEXT OF KIN

your name the one
I wrote down when asked

your name the one I carried
around just in case

your phone number I knew
better than my own

your's never did change
as I moved around

way back from jump
always the same eventually

no matter the friends I found
you were next of kin

Two or More Conversations

—

1
I wanted to walk
right up to you
and tell you
I want to fuck you

instead I told you
I love you
now ain't that loving
you baby huh huh

2
let me get this straight
first you lied to me
now you mad at me
because I believed you

3
someone made up the truth
and called it art
that's not true I said

4
to my left she's reading
a book on feminism
making notes in the margins
to my right two women talking
about their boyfriends
all three are pissed

5
inner voice inner child
too many voices
a new voice replied

Money Mouth

you'd be surprised what money can do
fund a cure bridge dry rivers

what can love buy but more charity
trade barter it's all money

money's like guns
no bad money just bad people

people don't mind you
got money as long as they can beg

borrow steal work like a dog for it
and I'd love you better

if we had enough money to say
we don't need money

POSTCARD FROM JAMAICA

Halfway Tree to Mona
on the minibus
Friday night fish fry
Papine Kingston JA style
man selling Red Stripe
cold or warm (*Gleaner* finished)
the walk back to my room
Barry G's on the radio
talking to Brooklyn
next day slept late
the afternoon
breeze on time
not Jamaican time
not CP time
I could set my clock
by that breeze
sweeping through my window
a sailor's dream breeze
which I wake up to
like water undulating
across my face

The *Gleaner* is the major newspaper in Jamaica;
Halfway Tree and Mona are sections in
Kingston; minibuses are privately owned public
transportation; and Barry G a DJ on the JBC. CP
time needs no explanation

Two Moments

1
bones bird small
toothpicks for a dinosaur
primitive feelings
harden thaw disappear
your sunlit wrists are crows
your smell beneath my fingernails
the manicurist complains
there are no civil rights for dinosaurs

2
like a Sunday feast
this morning's blood
your friend
and mine is welcome here
it's our monthly armistice
outside it's raining
church bells toll

RADIO MEMORIES
for *Wolfman Jack*

Sweet Jesus in all his names
made you want to be

that woman's lover that man's friend
according to the top ten

Monday through Sunday jazz
gospel r&b reigned like rap try today

until I brought Bach into the house
everyone thought I was cool

Joko Symphony Sid a few radio heroes
WNJR kept me company hours

more affordable than black & white TV
and not nearly as rare

as stereo record players
radio was my cyberspace my socket

to the world so much so
a home without a radio was nowhere

that's why the electric bill
had to be paid right after the rent

why transistors were a temporary fix
had a car without a radio

you might as well walk
static free twenty four seven Come

Sunday God's in the house
Nowadays you got to DJ for yourself

Funk Heart

center the low beat
the one the others depend upon
for solace

for sanity's sake
keep the growl to a minimum
not too mum

the rain the poet heard
the womb time
a happy childhood in tune

singing skin to skin
the bare bone luck of love
turning corners

the poet to his mistress
whose back in their lovemaking
becomes a drum

a gentle hand on a breast
oh drum mother
black rose of the mind

the mother's milk of rhythm
the funk heart
peace the only applause

Namesake

I was named after the doctor
who delivered my mother from me

my birth certificate says
I was born colored the date weight

the stamp of the old City Hospital
the doctor's fancy scribble

my parents' names in bright blue ink
biblical nickname proof

I could always unfurl a new name
like Saul became Paul

but what was the good doctor after
I asked my mother once

and she sighed what's the matter
you don't like your name

and we both laughed
it was the last time I saw her alive

WORD

cool's replaced okay
as the all-American word

just be cool for Jesus
did I hear right

cool's gone kosher
laid back easy on the larynx

okay's all right for a state
groovy as in a groove

became a rut soon after liftoff
copacetic's passé

as the next previous generation
okie dokie's so dorkie

it's almost irie
solid passed into oblivion

cool stayed universal
one of the two most admired

temperatures worldwide
moderate calming in a word cool

II

KINDNESS

is like a fairy tale
voluptuous clouds phallic
apparitions fallacies of delight
misty fables

like the kind a dirty
young man
would write if he wanted to
fool the censors

mothers and salespersons
with symbols
what's it like you ask as if
I knew kindness well

I can only guess
it's like the wonderful cumulus
I'll meet one morning
on my way to the supermarket

meanwhile I'm only thinking
of something wholly
imaginary but it's impossible
to explain

except by saying
I hugged the fog and enjoyed
every chill
of it just like I do you

and I hope
we have a nice ending
and that it's fun getting there
though we might be sad

TWO CHILDREN'S SONGS

1
poor apple cider
you can't get anyone high
you taste so good
I wish you were champagne
poor apple cider
I been sitting here thinking
what am I gonna do
you taste so doggone good
but you can't get anyone high
poor apple cider poor apple cider

2
corduroy is my brother
he whistles when we walk together
corduroy's soft as wet grass
keeps me warm and never itchy
corduroy's my brother
the only skin I like better
is my skin

STORIES (I)

mother met father after arriving
from Virginia with her sister
she was seventeen when they married

my father's father was white
but daddy didn't like white people
said they treated him and my aunt mean

after their mama died
when they had to go live with their
daddy's people who were white

which was strange since
we were taught to treat everybody decent
daddy read the paper and Bible

every day till he dropped dead
massive heart attack day we moved
into our new house

I like to keep to myself since then
I guess except for my son
mother lives with the brother nearest me

less than a mile from me
she lives to see her grandson graduate
medical school. Now I can finish my degree

Blues Seminar

I want to believe in God so I do
I want to ride lightning and stay grounded

years ago a white man yelled NIGGER at me
I shouted back your mama likes it

good friends don't borrow love
wallflowers are patsies

butterflies can't rest on their laurels
I want to stand still like a hummingbird

but people I can't let my shadow
take all the blame for my poor side

the blues are a truth serum
after listening to a lying sermon

America gave the Negro the blues
don't you let anybody tell you different

MAMA'S BOY BLUES

I told my inlaws I told my outlaws
see how one hand treats the other

sometimes the people closest to you
turn out to be so far away

you ever seen a grown woman cry
her face lonely as one eye

I told my inlaws I told my outlaws
something's got to give

it's time I gave up the ghost
you never seen a grown woman cry

like she's an angel calling you home
she rocks she rocks

I told my inlaws I told my outlaws
you ever make your woman cry

like your daddy did your mama
nobody cry pretty not even a baby

CHURCH

together we're better than lunacy
the quiet darkness of your left hand
disappearing in the night
beneath between becoming the darkness

love only the two of us can make three
till then let's roll our pallets up
talk jazz like gods
I call your name in my sleep

and your magnolia mouth answers
in the forgetful forest
my fear my faith my ace of blues
we make love like we're going to church

TONIGHT

a month ago as the calendar flies
I was born to a sweet woman
my father must have loved some forty
years ago when both were younger

than I am now (for eight children
lived to adulthood one dying
on the highway one on a one-night stand
beaten and left for dead)

both parents have long since joined
the ancestors and I think about the time
I overheard my father laugh
what's the matter you used to like it

and I try to imagine my mother
opening to receive my father's power
for I want to honor seed and flower
stem and root by making love tonight

Through a
Plate-Glass Window

women trying on hats
a passerby
vain voyeur on the blvd

a sunlit window
women twirling light
into their world a glance

a chance to be ignored
as they dance
only for each other

their laughter
the pane of glass
the distance to their joy

only thing better ·
than dancing
watching others dance

THE PLEA

Take me home
To your living room
Ride me in your limousine

You got
Brains pretty mama
Yea that put mine to shame

If you leave
Me I gonna swallow
The ocean and drown my troubles

You got
A good job good looks
And you live in a big fine house

I'm a poor boy
Poorer than your mice
Dumber than your butler's maid

But I can
Sing you the alphabet
Backwards and make you forget it

I'll love you
Like a candle melts
Slow and hot (just like charcoal)

Cause I need
You like I do a medicine
And my soul's too black to swim

Strange Fruit

nobody I knew died
nobody alive I recognized

again I recount the body count
a mantra I can't let go

another horror of human error
whimsical as God's will

then the news broke
even the weather woman

was mischievous misleading
at best promising

there were survivors
I was off by several lives

outside it's still snowing (inside
I'm listening to Billie Holiday)

NOTES ON POVERTY

both eat envy with greed
both loathe poverty

except the poverty
of the saints who choose

their poverty: worst
than being poor is being

indifferent to poverty
if poverty's the worst thing

that can happen to you
you're already poor

FOR THE TOLL TAKER

I drive down your tunnel
With my lights out
The dark grabs me
And tells me its story
I listen and repeat it
Until it's my story
My power descends
The dark is moist
With expectations
I turn off the motor
Coasting for the exit
That has to happen
A lifetime from now

STORIES (2)

some men like that she said
he could be drunk
and you'd never know it

unless he fell asleep
could take him anywhere
funeral a picnic my whole family

liked him almost as much as I did
and he kept a good job
only thing was he dressed country

you can't have everything
which explains why
I wonder about him sometimes

III

THE BIG-FOOT CLUB

welcome to the big-foot club
no size under twelve

the motion on the floor
to induce women

not for politics
fear comes in all sizes

like pride in body parts
genes or God

I know folks who squeeze
their sevens into fives

who wants to be average
you tried to be like everybody else

welcome to the big-foot club
let the dancing begin

The Better Fiction

love suspends disbelief
demands suspense

mystery truth
melodrama comedy

more poetry than prose
like flying south

to meet the spring
love desires pure poetry

it's the myth
it's the plot we die for

BONGO

this fella who says rhythm
it's not so important
he don't know polka from mambo

take physics it has to be exact
and philosophy too
no hip cat can do that

even if he study xyz
what's so rare about rhythm
can you breath eat make love to it

then I figure out the problem
how he calypso bop
do the wild thing when his science

still counting sheep
he don't know titty from cancan
he don't know how to dance

whole dance with just the eyes
and he say rhythm easy
like he the Pope

PICTURE OF A MAN

He draws a man,
bright swirls of red.
And I say give me a tree.
He points to the middle
of his red and says,
"There's a tree!"
Tonight without complaining
he goes off to sleep
asking why in his storybook
the big boats have little
boats. He shouts
goodnight: I ask if he wants
the light out—
he says no, that he can't see
without the light.
A different excuse than
last night when he was plain scared.
Later I turn off the light—
his face soft as a breast.
And I know then what another man
meant when he said
maybe I could have loved
better
but I couldn't have loved more.
I thought of a woman
like that once.
This child is all I have left.

MEAD

except for making love
cultivating some intoxicant
was our first love

but the mind after
domesticating the wild beast
looked to the hereafter

and sought human solace
and pledged moderate inebriation
and so lace

swords pants and skirts
the finer things
like differences under skirts

and not to piss where one lies
all manner of manners
how numbers lie

to measure the moon
to harvest love instead of wine
curse the moon

this we did and do
in counting our brief pleasures
what else are we to do

Oreo

all metaphors aside
a bossman's no master: a slave
can't quit or get fired from slavery

which might be what that white woman
meant when she said
her old man told his bossman

her voice so full of North Carolina
style chopped barbecue
she was so herself I had to smile

her face wrinkled from tobacco
booze and good living
a downhome white woman so unlike

that white woman panhandling
in Baltimore who asked me for a quarter
before seeing my face

then she turned away ashamed and said
she still white no shit
her exact words

FACTS

The Sunday N.Y. *Times* reports
Italians (in Italy)
eat on the average 60 lbs. of pasta
per year; in the U.S.A. (Americans) 18 lbs

Further research confirms the rumor: African
Americans eat two times more
Fried Chicken on average
than other Americans

Meanwhile across the street
in the church parking lot (today's
Saturday) the neighborhood kids bundled up
for the chilly fall play stickball
a summer game

Luckily I have all my senses
intact (with the help of my new bifocals)
all except common sense
a luxury all over the world according
to my mother who is now in heaven Amen

So many FACTS more FACTS than insects
more FACTS than bugs (believe it or not) so many FACTS
in fact that I am often confused
Blind to feelings Deaf to intuition Dumb to mascara
Survey says: people consume more FACTS
than are good for them

BIO
a book report on the great poet Anon

Aesop was not Anon nor Dr. Seuss
Or the Brothers Grimm
Nor Sophocles or Walt Disney

Anon hung out in Africa Russia Japan
Greenland Cuba India
Anon could have been a woman

Anon sang beer songs love songs
Odes to God and babies
And X-rated dreams in every dialect

Anon never wrote a screenplay
Nor any top forty hits
Sometimes a prophet Anon's no god

Though Anon was on the Ark
Telling flood stories
Anon's so bad I want to be anonymous

BLUES

I have no use for nothing
Nothing don't do a thing for me

I love my race I love to dance
Seven come eleven I'm going to heaven

I punched out the time clock
Women never love you for your money

Some crumbs worth more than cakes
I do nothing very well

Doing nothing's hard to do
I say I was born to play and lay

Raise hell and still go to heaven
Some people's crumbs worth more than cakes

LIKEWISE

same here doesn't do it
likewise sees itself
coming and going wise like

likewise like kickass or eventide
deserves to be one word
a.k.a. like wisdom

imagine what likewise
tells us about us
like fuck's old, a commonplace

circa Anglo Saxon Celtic
fuck or fuck you
also plays the role of an adverb

likewise is like you know
smartass two words become one
likewise is like wise

Two Songs

1
my dead their breath human
to the finish

their sighs light as whispers
brief as sweet sex

we die too slow too fast
never too smooth

oh my dead die so well
they scare me

2
two is the lowest number
one the only one

two words to turn a phrase
two sounds to twist

a tongue to whistle
two to verify one to survive

whose mind will I be on
like you on mine

two is the lowest number
one the only one

IV

Blind Date with a Voice

Shine met a girl named Glow who stole
The night from the moon.
She's a lady DJ and Shine liked to imagine her
Nude as she sounded,

Sitting naively before the mike,
Her waterfalling voice flowing thru the air-
Ways into Shine's house.
And Shine longed to kiss her voice.

Sundown he followed her steps
And Glow thought Shine was her shadow.
Together in the elevator they spoke
And got off speaking at the hundredth floor.

There he carved her name on a cloud
And promised to take her to see John Coltrane.
Then Shine jumped out the window
For he had to be home before his mother opened the door.

PICTURE HER VOICE

The graph of Glow's voice
Was as shapely as her shape.

Like the swaying of her hips
Her speech has curves.

The wind blows up her dress
And feels like a thousand fingers.

The arch of her small foot
Is as fine as any in Notre Dame.

She just wanted to be held
Even if it meant she had to hold herself.

HOMING

The water's wonderful there
And the women aren't bad
Neither when you look at them
Twice, but the blame

Lies in that glass from the tap
For making me want to go back.
I went looking for where they get
It from but I got a ticket

For speeding; and when I said
I'm Mister Shine, a black ghost,
Cop said that's too bad.
Glow I was lost.

But my sermon is about the water,
How it's precious like family
When you wanting something familiar.
It made me happy—

It taste like baby's breath,
Like dew. I never knew sweeter water.
But I'm a spook's spook; I stole
This story from a dead man's mouth.

He was a preacher from Virginia
Who before he expired said:
Somewhere there's a well of sweet water.
Somewhere in Ohio or maybe Carolina.

TRAVELING IS SO ENLIGHTENING

The Golden Gate Bridge reminds Shine
Of the wire he had in his mouth as a child.
Gums forlorn, bowlegged teeth,
And braces until he was twenty-one.

Shine travels through Nebraska,
The land as flat as his nose.
One ocean behind him like a squaw,
Up south singing a song as he meditates:

If you never wash your neck
And dirt collects
Thick as a second skin,
Then you won't have to worry.
You won't get a red neck.

Shine drives a limousine.
A man's car, Shine whispers,
Should be as comfortable as his living room.
Smoking a reefer thick as his thumb,

He flicks his ashes
In every state and arrives
In New Orleans looking for a new Dream Book.
But he returns to Harlem in one piece.

Shine, Shine where you been—
Back and around the world again.
I've seen things that best remain unsaid.
One sure thing I learned: KISS
ASS and you shall receive.

Debating with J.C.

Shine met Jesus at the well
And said how do you do?
I'm all right, sinner, how about you?
You ready for hell?

No, Shine said. That water's
Too bitter, don't suit
My taste. Life is rough enough,
Why go down yonder?

Lord, please grant me a parole?
Nay, Shine. You been unhappy anyway.
Why stay another day?
Plus you too old

For lust, too young for love.
Shine confessed his time
Was spent drinking and gambling.
So God sent a dove.

But Shine wanted a crow.
It's good to know Shine won
The debate without a knife or a gun.
My shadow won't grow.

It's the cross I bear.
Forty days without any women
Was an omen. Now
My vision is clear as desert air.

THE DANCERS

At the party
High and low Shine meditates
On the state of hearing
The bleary-eyed look of love's last chance
The tyranny of dance
Before the behinds bump and rub
Before the hostess unscrews the bulb
And slowly exhausted
Rests against the shoulder of the night
While he happy to just be alive
And high
Watches the dark bodies in the dark
And listens

SICK UNTO DYING

People stood around his bed
As if to keep warm;
And his women folded their hands
Into steeples
While his cronies turned
Their faces toward the walls.

They were all expecting his soul
To rise up like a red balloon
Before their eyes.
For they wanted their faith made
Visible; and they knew Shine
Would go out in style.

Sick unto dying he was losing air.
And he knew his jive
Had got him busted by the law
Which no court on earth
Could overrule. Brothers
Something unkind was coming down.

But when they shut St. Peter's
Gate in his face
Shine said, "I've been triple-crossed
By the trinity.
First I was born unto dying,
And now I got to live again in hell."

POSTCARD FROM COLORADO

Shine told Glow
Your hands are like aspens
Kinetic on the Colorado hillside.
The mute lighter palm
The darker loud back hand
Flashing before me.
And after the stillborn monologue
They fall to your waist
As if the wind had died suddenly with no
Thought of returning.

DRUM CRAZY

The year of the drummer
He fell into a coma.

Sulking, he couldn't turn his
Cotton into silk.

All he remembered was
The drummer's hands, the thin

Fabric, delicate
As a chin, the speed and precision

Of each hit tightening
His stomach like hunger or worry.

But still he was greedy enough
To ask for more.

Until tongue-tied
Shuddering like a cold motor

He found a chair
And dozed off full of shock.

Delirious, dreaming
Of his bout against the drums.

DAFFODIL GHETTO

Shine among the daffodils
Is uneasy; hovering
Like a cop

In Harlem

He beckons to the wind
Whose prophecy insults him.
But he doesn't grieve

Over the green stems
The injury cut by the massive
Yellowing plain:
All streaking
Brash as a mob of coeds.

For he's the witness
To the confusion and perceives evil, anger

As folly:

His fate's a nuisance.
He goes home gloomy, moaning
About moonlit rain
Falling

Falling—
How he could be alive
And nobody know it.

SHINING

Don't treat me so bad
You the best man
I ever had.

You hurt me so good
I wouldn't leave
You if I could.

I drift like driftwood
From shore to shore.
Each man I love
Takes a little bit more.

On First Hearing
Sonny Rollins Live

Shine heard the tune.
Again the myth
Made flesh; the memory
Spins and records.

The club lights darken
As if to honor now
The tenor man who has come
Home singing.

Eyes shut, Shine forgets
His glass of gin.
As though in church
He listens.

He wants the tenor man
To be his Messiah.
He wants to be saved
From the well-lit silence.

The integrity of the song
Is a revelation,
Amplified. But the lights
Come on. Shine blinks

An angry what?
But it's closing time.
It was a sermon in stereo.
Yes time to go home.

THE NIGHT IS A MIRROR

Shine and the night became
Identical twins.
But Glow was jealous
Of the two brothers and sought

To sever the bond.
Cast in the same die, they shared
The same hurting lore
Of loneliness. Indivisible—

Invisible in the dark.
Shine hides behind the horizon.
He creeps across the bridge, hesitates,
Then stares at hell below.

Come home, Glow demands.
He talks to himself, whistles sad
Songs and hints
Of moonless universal insomnia.

You can't see him.
He's everywhere surrounding you.
Your shadow swallows you.
It's your fear; it's quiet. It's Shine

Ms. Glow

1
Glow was delicious
Perfectly Benin
A mask of wooden moods.

But soft and warm
As a piece of coal fresh
Out the fire.

You could crush her
In your hands
If you wanted to.

2
Her mouth was curved
Into a moist grin

Like a canoe
Just out the water.

She could row you to Africa
With one slow protruding kiss.

DREAMS AND DEEDS

His dream had intermissions
Eons too long
As if his lengths

Had shorted out
And he tried back-stepping
But he stumbled hard

His will ran dry
His favorite solvent wasn't
Happening

And nothing between sets
As he waited
For the turnings

Outward he was mostly
Only red-eyed
And just the same Shining